SCRUB TECH
COLORING BOOK

THIS BOOK BELONGS TO

____

Keep Calm
and
Stay
Sterile

I LIKE
PEOPLE
under general
Anesthesia

SCRUB
life

I GAVE UP
MY LIFE
TO LEARN
HOW TO
SAVE
yours

BEHIND EVERY GREAT
surgeon
IS AN EVEN GREATER
SCRUB TECH

Essential
AF

SCRUB TECH.
HEALER.
FUCKING
LEGEND.

BE NICE TO ME
I'M A
Surgical
Tech
I KEEP DOCTORS
FROM
KILLING YOU

I'M A
SURGICAL
TECH
WHAT'S YOUR
SUPER
POWER?

LOOK AT YOU
BECOMING A
SCRUB
TECH
and Shit

WORLD'S
Okayest
SCRUB
TECH

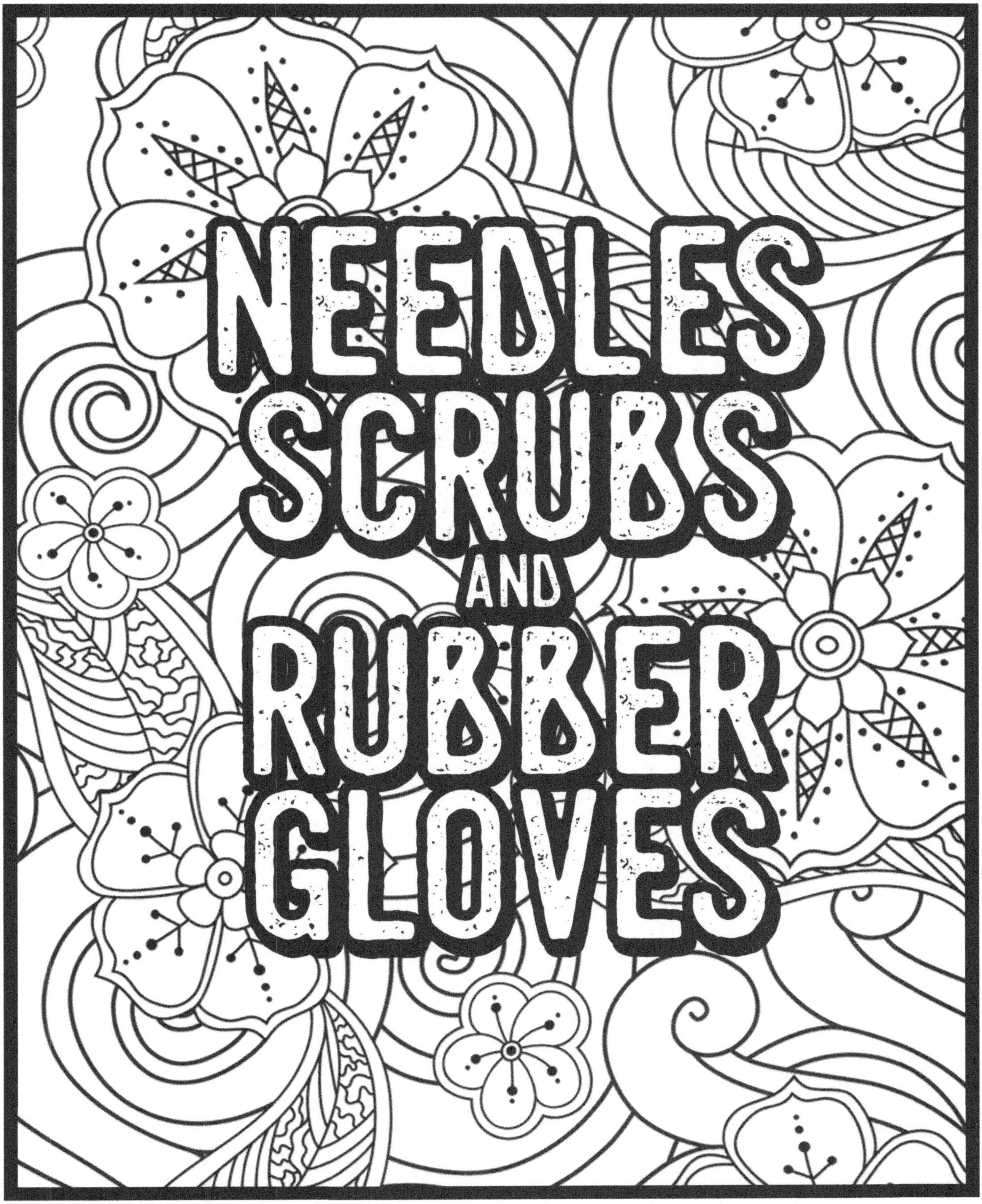
NEEDLES
SCRUBS
AND
RUBBER
GLOVES

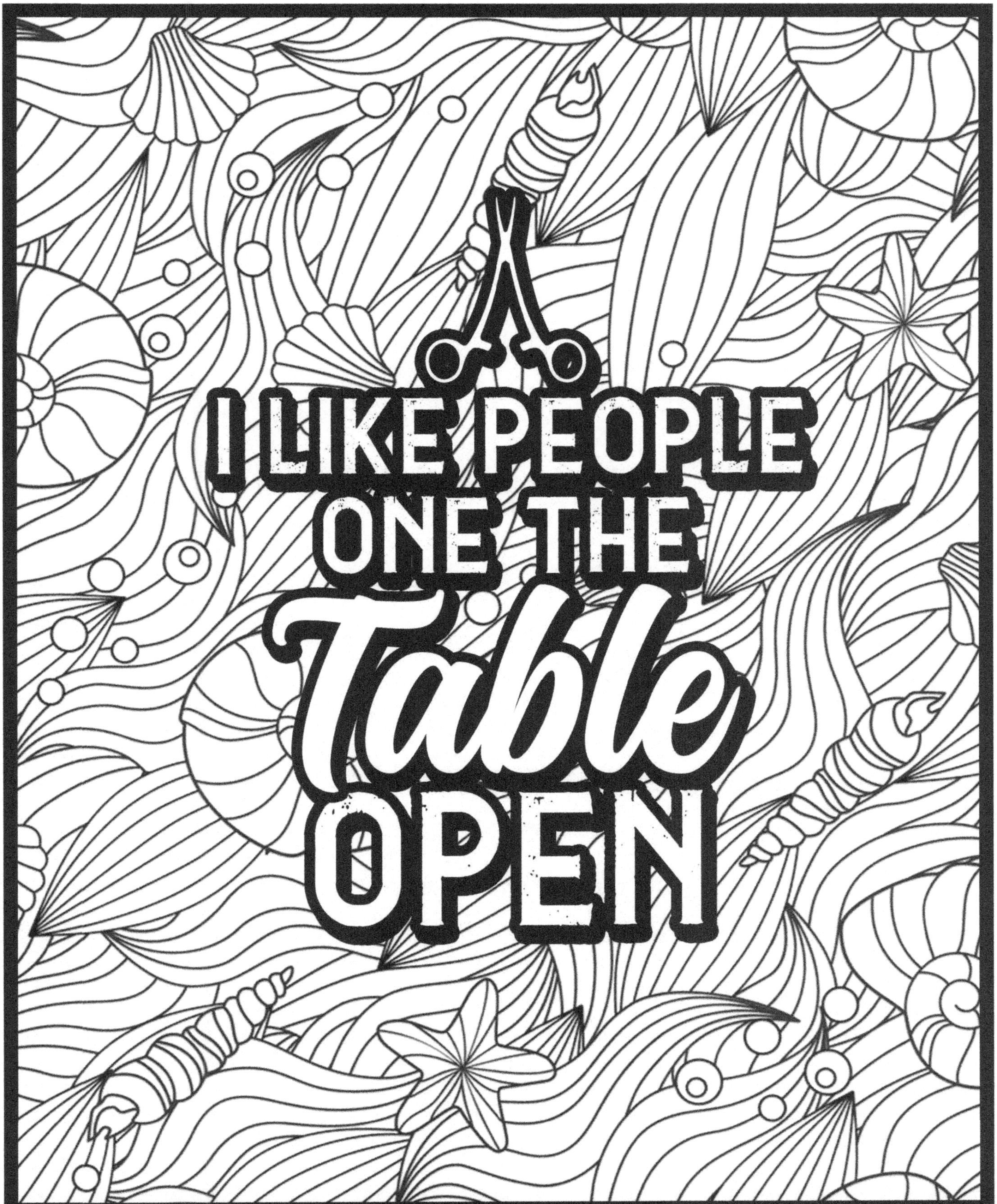
I LIKE PEOPLE
ONE THE
Table
OPEN

THIS
SCRUB
TECH
NEEDS A
MOTHER
FUCKING
Nap

IT'S A BEAUTIFUL
Day
TO SAVE
Lives

it takes lots
of Sparkles
to be a
Scrub
Tech

Trauma
QUEEN

Eat.
Sleep.
Operate.
Repeat.

Foul
Mouthed
Scrub
Tech

I SCRUB
I DRINK
and
I KNOW
THINGS